Very practical insights that will transform
your marriage/relationship.

(Revised Edition)

DELADEM K. LOGLO

Copyright © 2016 Deladem K. Loglo

ISBN 13:   978-9988-2-3062-3

Author: **Deladem K. Loglo**

+233202019599

Published by

Virtue Publications

+233500077488/+233247927551

(virtuepublicatios@gmail.com)

<u>Design & Print (First Edition)</u>

Dot Concepts **(+233) 244 182 390, (+233) 233 355 621**
Email: **dotsconcept@gmail.com**

DEDICATION

*T*his book is dedicated to all who are committed to making sure their relationships and/or marriages succeed no matter what, and making it as God desired it to be.

APPRECIATION

To God the giver of wisdom, understanding and Insight, to my dear wife Aseye for her love and all the lessons I have learnt in marriage.

I also want to say a big thank you to all those who contributed to this book by responding to the questions I posed; to Dr. Vanessa Tetteh, Nally, Keziah and Mr. & Mrs. Brown for editing; to all those who taught me via observation; and to my incredible children - Sedinam, Nuku and Eyram, for teaching me another dimension in life.

AGREEMENT

$\mathcal{I}$f you treat this as an ordinary book, you will miss it and learn nothing.
kindly worship God and pray intensely before you start reading this book.

Pray in this direction:
• Ask for the blood of Jesus to wash you clean, and purify you as you come before him.

• Pray for a specific encounter with God, and ask for the presence of the holy spirit to lead you in a spirited search.

• Plead with God to open your eyes so that you will perceive wondrous things out of this   book that will take you to the next level in your marriage / relationship.

• Finally, pray for God to reveal unto you what

you need to do to make your marriage/ relationship what god desired it to be.

Thank God for answering your prayers in the precious name of Jesus Christ.

Kindly place your hand on the sketch on the right, and say this prayer after me:

Daddy, I honor you. I come into agreement with you, and precious Holy Spirit. I declare as in Mathew 18: 19 – "*... if two of you agree on earth about anything they ask, it will be done for them by my Father in heaven*" ESV, that may my relationship blossom. May there be transference as I read this book in the precious name of Jesus Christ.

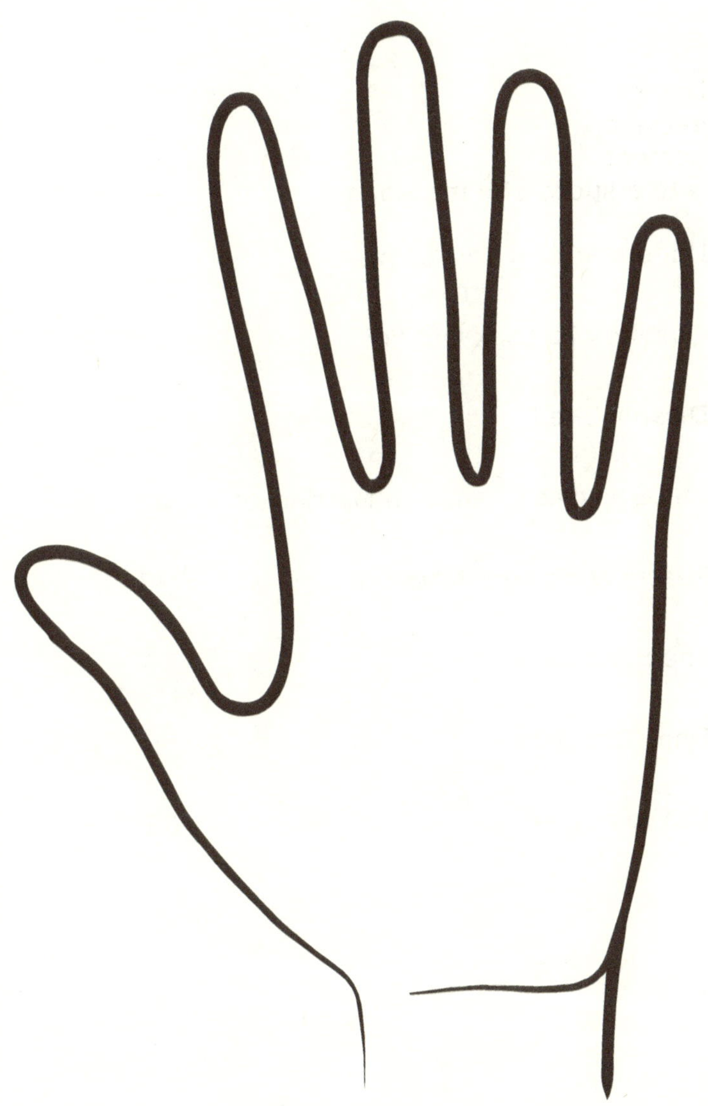

CONTENTS

KEYS TO A SUCCESFUL MARRIAGE.

Show appreciation: Happily married couples show appreciation to each other even for the least gesture of love, and thoughtfulness. Nothing undermines love more than being taken for granted. When your partner does not show appreciation for the good things you do, it is extremely difficult to keep up the good work.

James Ebo Whyte (Uncle Ebo Whyte).

Roverman Productions Limited.

Marriage is a decision, and is about commitment. It is not just based on feelings as most people think. Understanding one another makes the marriage grow stronger.

Mrs. Flora Sackey, Marriage Counsellor

To enjoy successful and thriving marriages, both partners must be saved, apply grace in their marriage, respect the principle of "the two becoming one", and ensure that they invest in companionship.

Mensah Seneadza, Coca Cola Equatorial Guinea

Loving God more than yourself or your spouse; Striving to be close to God makes you closer to each other. Being open and honest with each other... not holding back or hiding. Praying together daily. Going out for date nights. Husband being a real spiritual head of his wife and family. Husband and wife raising their children in a 'no compromise' way.

Dr. Vanessa Tetteh, Host Consult

Marriage is indeed a good relationship between loving couples and it is upon this premises we give this encouragement. It can flourish when tendered with care and maintained. Patient wise effort over time will yield a good marriage. It is an institution ordained by God and therefore, for it to work best, one needs to go back to the one who created and ordained it. The first and foremost is when Gen. 2 :24 tells us that there must be a leaving, a cleaving and becoming one flesh. If these commands are not heeded to, one could envisage problems.

Create your own home. Continue your courtship, i.e revive the courtesies of courtship in your marriage- out love each other. You could not have come together by accident. The bible says, "Can two walk together unless they agree? (Amos 3:3). The two of you have chosen to live together by agreement. There is nothing like " I made a mistake in marrying you". "NEVER". You never made a mistake- keep on giving each other respect, love, time and attention.

Communicate effectively- skills such as active listening, paying attention to your spouse's feelings, fighting fair (no blame game) and expression of appreciation must be learned and put into practice. Never retire for the night angry with each other, stay positive and don't focus on the everyday little irritations from your spouse or talk endlessly about them. Commitment should not be left to chance; it means working hard and becoming creative. It bonds a couple together. It is the resolve to keep investing in the relationship and to prevent distractions from destroying the union. One essential ingredient you need is *Common Values.*

If the values are significantly different, it's a red flag for the couples. It doesn't matter how well the couples communicate, their basic life orientation will prevent constant opportunities for conflict but having common values will facilitates conflict resolution. Hold fast your dreams together, the future is a blank page waiting for you to write your life story on therefore, be reminded that your marriage is a story being told, end it well but not half way.

Take a little time for yourself and think if everything that you hope for will go right, where you would like to be, how you will be living and what you will be doing in three or five years to get going, but to start today. May you be encouraged by his quotation, "The wind of grace blows all the time. All we need to do is set our sails". Never give in. Never, Never, Never. Sir Winston Churchill (1874- 1965). We want you to be in the wonderment that there is great energy in the human soul that drives you two to better yourselves and improve the fortunes of your relationship, families and societies/communities. Indeed, we know of no greater force on earth. God should be the center of your marriage and keep tapping from his strength. Never cease to pray together and guard your thoughts.

Dr. and Mrs. Romeo & Betty Aygapong.

1

UNDERSTANDING THE GAME

"Husbands, likewise, dwell with them with understanding, giving honor to the wife, as the weaker vessel, and as being heirs together of the grace of life, that your prayers may not be hindered"

I Peter 3:7 (NKJV)

A few months ago, I was going through a few personal issues resulting from the phases in marriage and I asked God, "Why am I going through these challenges?" He said to me calmly, "I thought you wanted to be a Personal Development Consultant? You have to experience everything, so that you can confidently teach others."

This connects with what a wise man once said, "If you claim you are a general, show me your scars."

I have seen so many marriages collapse, others existing but dead, and others dead on arrival. I dare say that marriage is indeed an unending university education with no graduation. It is a lifelong learning process which never ends. It is said that when you think you have understood your spouse, another set of demand sets in. The goalpost keeps changing.

The picture below from an anonymous person on WhatsApp sums it up:

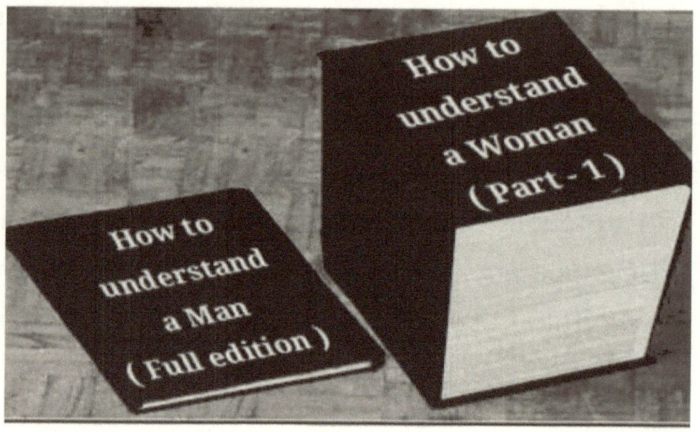

Marriage is a high maintenance relationship. You don't buy a new car, fuel it, and expect it to run without problems. Marriages, no matter how great or simple, encounter some problems, in one area or the other.

Observing from afar, it always seems easy to hop into a senior position in an organization with the belief that you can do even better. Most people face reality when they experience the role and realize it is not as easy as they thought.

Likewise, marriage is very nice but you need to learn the basics in selecting your partner and actually staying enlisted (married), enjoying and not enduring.

Examining the life of   elderly people we have visited lately, it has dawned on me quite clearly that after a few years, all your children will be gone and all you will have will be your spouse, not a house or a car or any other gadget. Consequently, we need to work on our marriages and make them far better than they are now.

Warren Bennis, in his book "Becoming a Leader" said, "*Marriage offers 90% of all your support in life - happiness and fulfillment so choose wisely*" But the question is: how many people choose wisely?

I want to indicate that this book is absolutely my opinion; from observation and reflection, experiences, and data collected from both married and unmarried, notes written after counseling others, etc.

Although not exhaustive, I believe it will expose people who are about getting married to some qualities to look out for in selecting their spouses. Additionally, I touch on what happens if you are already married but missed out on any of the qualities mentioned. I go further to elaborate on reasons why spouses change in marriage. I then proceed to suggest ways by which marriages on the verge of breaking down could be reactivated, rejuvenated and revived in order to avoid self-destruction. In an unconventional way, I bring to bare spiritual issues that impact marriages unknowingly, and sum up with my final thoughts on marriage.

This book was purely written by inspiration with only practical insights which will assist any serious- minded person who is committed to his or her marriage or other relationship.

May the Spirit of God rush upon you while you read and meditate on the insights revealed in this book, in the precious name of Jesus Christ!

2

QUALITIES TO LOOK OUT FOR

"Successful people make right decisions early and manage those decisions daily".

-John Maxwell.

*I*n his book **"Today Matters"**, John Maxwell submitted that "successful people make right decisions early and manage those decisions daily"

In my opinion, there is no clear-cut requirement in the selection of a spouse. Everyone has different criteria, however, there are some basics that cut across. The list below will serve as a guide, but not in order of priority:

a. **Patience**

With patience a ruler may be persuaded, and a soft tongue will break a bone. Proverbs 25:15.

Whoever you want to marry requires a bit of patience in his or her life. It makes a lot of difference in relationships. This quality can be developed if it is lacking or inadequate.

I propose that at least one partner must be extremely patient

b. **Someone who shares or cares**
Nobody wants to marry a stingy or selfish

person. Let me give you a free tip. Most prospective spouses observe each other when they are dating. What do you do when you both alight from a vehicle or when you go out to eat? Make an attempt to pay the bill and this must be done genuinely not pretentiously. There are times that you need to insist to pay.

Doing this will automatically earn you some points into your LOVE account.

c.   **Respect** - not only for spouse-to-be, but to   siblings, parents and other family members.

d.   **Common interests/hobbies**
This is one of the most important qualities in the selection of a spouse. Indeed, having common interests / hobbies enhances communication in the relationship and strengthens the relationship.

If you truly love someone and want to be with the person, seek to develop an interest in what s/he loves to do and take part actively. This will fumigate parasites in the relationship.

e. Does the other person truly love you and not for any ulterior motive?

This is a whole topic by itself because it has a lot of shades.

f. Sense of humor

Humor releases tension in a relationship or home. If you are not humorous look for someone who can make you laugh and seek to do same.

There is a saying that all work and no play makes Jack a dull boy …..

g. Intelligence - you need someone who can stimulate you intellectually.

h. Integrity / truthfulness

Never marry a liar. I believe, a liar can change but ??? Please think twice about it.

i. A good cook.

This is also a very important one. Females are looking for gentlemen who know how to cook, and vice versa. Most females are now taking up short courses in catering to make themselves more marketable.

You may visit some online sites, example Allrecipes.com for assistance.

j. **Maturity**

This can be described in the words of a wise man as the ability to laugh at you. When you ponder over certain issues and wonder whether you indeed did them, you can consider yourself as growing.

I mean that the heir, as long as he is a child, is no different from a slave, though he is the owner of everything.

Galatians 4:1

k. **Compatibility** - can be worked at with commitment.

However considering issues such as blood type, sickling and purpose help in avoiding unnecessary work.

l.   **Indescribable characteristic of chemistry**

This embodies effective and enjoyable communication, something unique about your partner that attracts you or turns you on, also known as 'electric shocks'. In some cases, this can be either physical or behavioral.

m. **A responsible person**

Pastor Mensa Otabil once said, "If you can't lace your shoes, can you take care of someone else?" All he wanted to say was that, for a relationship to be successful, each spouse must be responsible or be able to take care of themselves first so as not to be a burden.

n. **Share the same faith**

This is very essential, because it has a lot of implication on your spiritual life, children, and grandchildren, just to mention a few. There are people who share the same faith but the woman could for instance be a Presbyterian, and the man a Charismatic. All these issues would have to be discussed, and firmed up before the marriage is blessed.

o. **Someone with a clear Vision and Purpose, who is focused and knows exactly what he or she wants in life or for the marriage.** Ignoring this can be very disastrous. There are spouses who do not have any vision for themselves, and become envious, and unsupportive when they realize their spouses are focused, and doing well. This, if not well handled, could eat up the joy in a hitherto sweet relationship.

Spouses are supposed to help each other grow. In order to do this well, there ought to be alignment of hearts and minds. Positive intent is key for this to occur. Any relationship where there is no alignment of purpose will definitely fail over time.

Couples must have a common goal and purpose which influences their worldview.

International Central Gospel Church, Ghana has a 20 Year Personal Development Plan online that can help in carving out focus for one's life, and that of your spouse. This can be done separately but each spouse must know what is in each other's plan so that they can grow together.

p. **A neat person**

This involves keeping oneself tidy and attractive at all times. The list of qualities to look for goes on and on. Others even look at beauty (beauty they say lies in the eyes of the beholder), shape of body, smile, etc. As indicated earlier, it varies per person.

Love is a very important foundation of marriage. It is important that you marry someone you love. Others claim that you can marry someone you like, and then try loving the person later.

To put it mildly, even the definition of love varies per person.

I Corinthians 13:4-7 gives very succinct definition of LOVE.

"4 Love is patient and kind; love does not envy or boast; it is not arrogant

5 or rude. It does not insist on its own way; it is not irritable or resentful;

6 it does not rejoice at wrongdoing , but rejoices with the truth.

7 Love bears all things, believes all things, hopes all things, endures all things"

A word of caution for those yet to marry; take your time and move slowly, and let no one put pressure on you to make an uncomfortable decision you cannot easily reverse.

Additionally, if you see a sign that you are not happy with about your prospective spouse, don't ignore it. Probe further, and ask yourself whether you can live with it, if the person does not change. If you think you can't, move on! This can only be possible if sex is avoided during courtship.

3

DISAPPOINTED?

"Character is not made out of sunshine and roses. Like steel, it is forged in fire, between the hammer and the anvil".

Ching Nin Chu, Thick Face, Black Heart

*T*here are times people marry and realize some of the things they truly require are missing or not in the right proportion.

This is where your character gets tested and refined. ColorDict defines character as an inherent complex of attributes that determines a person's moral, and ethical actions and reactions.

No human being is perfect so it is very normal not to have everything you want in a spouse. However, this is not an easy thing to accept, and live with.

Rexford was married to Ama for five years three months. Much of the experience was sweet and sour. But largely memorable.

One day, the man got fed up with the negativity of the wife. Everything he did was wrong in her sight. There were times he could make so much sacrifice just to make her happy. All she will do is to say something negative that will throw him off.

His organization transferred him to the UK as an expatriate. One day to his departure, He left a

Jewelry box by their bed for Ama. She saw the crystalike box. Before she even opened it, she presumably said eh! what is this ? She opened the box and saw a black stone and said "I knew this will not be anything worthwhile - such a black stone!"

She raised a cotton lining in the box and saw a letter. It was a letter from the court. She opened it and was shocked to the core by what she read. It was a divorce note from the court willing all their property to her (everything they had - five houses, 30 plots of land at strategic locations, a business, his SSNIT, end of service benefit, a Mercedes Benz E300 he used most of the time, while she kept the Lexus V8 - all 2016 Model) and a hand written note from the man.

"Honey,

I am relocating to the UK with the kids tomorrow for the next 10 years.

I have consistently worked on myself for you to accept me. You are so sweet (I know you understand me),beautiful, caring, full of ideas but extremely critical and always imagining evil for me which mars everything we have going. The best I do to please you is not up to your standard. Thanks for everything you have done for me and the children.

The stone you saw in the box is a token of my love for you. You are simply priceless! She chuckled (this dirty stone?) I have tried to communicate it to you in so many ways but you don't seem to see it. You have your own spectacles of LOVE which is so unique to you and not even biblical.

I trust that you find someone who can match your standard someday.

Love you

Broken Hearted Rex "

She shoved it off and showed no emotion.

After one week, she took the stone to a jewelry shop and realized the value of the dirty stone was $6.7 million - a rare black Diamond.

She had goose pimples all over. She started reflecting on how kind the Husband was despite his flaws (which he has admitted to and working on). She could admit He was seriously working on them .But she felt she was perfect, struggled to forgive all the time and always reminding him of his mistakes. She believed "you can't change anyone" and thus expected him to also live with her like that without she improving.

I was sad when the story was narrated to me and started asking myself what I would have done if I were in his shoes?

Morale of the Story

1. Appreciation and acceptance is key in the survival of any relationship

2. Every marriage has a cross. The cross could be as petty as how you brush your teeth or squeeze the toothpaste.

Paul who made so much impact in Ministry had a thorn in his flesh.

2 Corinthians 12:7(NET) even because of the extraordinary character of the revelations. Therefore, so that I would not become arrogant, a thorn in the flesh was given to me, a messenger of Satan to trouble me – so that I would not become arrogant.

Strong's Definition of thorn in the flesh - withered at the front, that is, a point or prickle (figuratively a bodily annoyance or disability): - thorn.

Thinking that marriage is all rosy is an illusion. Challenges will always come. What is important is how you handle them.

Napoleon Hill highlights a fact not known to many, in *"The Law of Success in Sixteen Lessons":* "The entire civilized world knows that the first two or three years of association after marriage are often marked by much disagreement, of a more or less petty nature. These are the years of "adjustment." If the marriage survives then it is more than apt to become a permanent alliance" Although he said the entire civilized world knows, it is not easy, and has never been.

Find below some of the reactions that may occur when some spouses realize something they wanted in the marriage is missing:

1.   Some resort to cheating

2.   Others spend long hours at work

3.   Frequent outings or long telephone

conversation with friends (Boys-Boys or Girls-Girls)

4.   Clock more hours on social media

5.   Indiscriminate sex life (multiple sexual

partners) Heb. 13:4

4 Let marriage be held in honor among all, and let the marriage bed be undefiled, for God will judge the sexually immoral and adulterous. (ESV)

1 Cor. 6:18

18 Flee from sexual immorality. Every other sin a person commits is outside the body, but the sexually immoral person sins against his own body. (ESV)

6. Absent mindedness, which impacts everything they do, including their careers

7. Leanness/Fatness- While some people grow fat when they are stressed, others grow lean due to bad eating habits

8. Rough/tired looking face (sometimes with lot of pimples - not always the case for everyone, though!)

9. Some females in this situation do not care about   makeup or looking good

10. Some make a lot of mistakes at work, or are unable to focus on anything

11. Drunkenness

1 Corin. 3:16-17

16 Do you not know that you are God's temple and

that God's Spirit dwells in you? 17 If anyone destroys God's temple, God will destroy him. For God's temple is holy, and you are that temple.(ESV)

If you feel like giving up, take a cue from John Maxwell, "Life is 10% what happens to me and 90% of how I react to it."

I can confidently say that most people get disappointed when they get married, and contemplate divorce at least once or twice. That notwithstanding, they acknowledge that marriage is a covenant between the couple, and God which must be held sacred. With a strong resolve not to divorce no matter what except as prescribed in the Bible, they commit to making sure they grow through personal development, and with God on their side, things fall in place with time.

"Events in life mean nothing if you do not reflect on them in a deep way, and ideas from books are pointless if they have no application to life as you live it,"- Robert Greene

4

CAN SPOUSES CHANGE IN MARRIAGE?

"....a positive attitude is important, but it is only part of the story. Understanding how to surmount pain, doubt and failure is a vital component in winning the game of life. So often we are so concerned with what makes us feel good and we forget   what makes us great".

-Ching Nin Chu, Thick Face, Black Heart

*T*his is an interesting question with a two pronged response. Spouses change for the better or for the worse. Others change permanently, others temporarily based on their circumstances. Some are able to recover, others don't.

Some of the key factors that cause the changes are:

1. Children

- *Delay in child birth*

When two people get married, their expectation is to get a child, which is not always the case.

There are times God delays it for reasons best known to him. The delay sometimes causes changes in some spouses. In extreme cases, other family members start names-calling and interfering. This breeds friction which, if not handled well, can result in a change in one or both spouses. Some might think, "Let me go, and get it elsewhere...."

- *With Children*

You appreciate your parents more when you start giving birth. The injection of children into a relationship impacts finances, sex life, attention from partner, physical appearance, among others. When this is not accepted and worked on consciously, a spouse might take hasty decisions based on the temporal situation.

2. Stress

Taking care of children in marriage is a nice thing. But it is also very demanding. Partners in this case become stressed out and could possibly change in their reaction to issues. Please take note, and take it easy.

3. Change in appearance

This occurs due to advancement in age, wrong eating patterns, habits, lack of exercise, health challenges, childbirth, etc. Some men for instance grow pot bellies whereas some women grow in size due to childbirth. If you marry for the wrong reason you will start having issues.

However, it is important that both spouses make an attempt to work on themselves to look good, and sexually attractive. If ignored, this can kill the passion in the relationship and cause a change in behavior.

4. In-laws

A very good relationship with your in-law(s), enhances the survival of the relationship, and vice versa. Some in laws are so nice that you are treated as their child.

You could even sleep on their beds or have a good conversation with them, and feel at home. I have been extremely fortunate in this area.

In some few instances, some in-laws in the bid to help their children, and ensure they stay married and happy, support in a lot of ways, and this can be misinterpreted as interference in some cases. Although there might be positive intent, due process must be followed. There must be mutual agreement on sensitive issues before in-laws are allowed to contribute.

Even if other extended family members should be cared for, it should be done in such a way that the needs of your new family (family of procreation) is not denied unnecessarily.

5. Finances / Money problems

Having too much or too little can cause changes in spouses. There is this joke of a lady who was asked which book had the greatest impact on her life, and she said, "My husband's cheque book." Trust me, some partners start avoiding discussions because they assume their spouses will give them headache, especially when there are things to be done and there is no money.

Some marriages adopt a joint account approach; others separate account but spend money together. Whatever the case, openness on financial matters helps a lot in resolving financial conflicts and building a healthy relationship. Won't it be strange to hear that your husband / wife has built a house somewhere without your knowledge?

6. Health challenges

Marriage is for the better or for the worse. Would you still love your spouse when he or she is plagued with a serious disease? Some people prove their love in such situations, whereas others become unsupportive, and abandon their spouses. It is important to remember when you take a particular course of action that, it could have been you.

7. Poor communication

Some spouses do not know how to talk at all. Any word from their mouths smells like "Zoomlion". What worsens this is if the spouse whose communication is poor does not accept it, and consciously attempt to work on it. Most people will do their best to hang in there, but if an attempt is not made to improve, or if the other spouse does not accept them as they are, the other party may change.

Communication affects everything in marriage.

8. Poor hygiene

Although love might still exist in a relationship, the consistent unkempt nature of a spouse could put the other off or cause their attitude to change. If there has been enough communication on personal hygiene (bathing, orals, unshaved or inadequately cleaned private parts, frequent candidiasis), the other spouse might consistently avoid sex or have it superficially without total involvement, and this will go a long way in hurting the relationship.

9. Lack of commitment or responsibility

In some cases, some spouses do not show that they are serious about the relationship no matter how much effort the other party puts in. This automatically triggers the question and reaction - why am I wasting my time? This definitely causes changes.

In any successful relationship, at least one spouse must be more committed and hopeful that things will work out.

An article I published on Facebook titled, "Keeping Trusting" makes this point so clear:

Kitson left Ama for the U.S. He promised going for just three months. Three months turned into four years. He changed his mind when he got there. While there, He wanted the wife to join him with their four children but she did not want to because she had a secured job as a Manager in one of the leading Banks in the country.She simply did not understand why she had to leave her job for menial jobs or felt he would not provide her needs or have too much power over her.

Six months went by, then a year. He started threatening he will get married if she did not join him. She stood her grounds ,family members came in but she refused to go. He indeed went ahead and got an elderly white woman to sort him out. lol

While the Husband was busy with the white lady, Ama was busy here growing and taking care of the children . She drew closer to God , involved herself in a lot of church activities, stayed away from men and continued taking care of their three girls and a boy. After all activities, She could stay alone in her room and cry all night.

Through all this, she had faith that something good was going to come out of the situation. Indeed, the last time I spoke to her, the husband was fully back in Ghana, apologized and had bought her a brand new Toyota Camry. Can you guess the inscription on his WhatsApp status? "My wife is a virtuous woman"

Ama has become a marriage counselor in her church, a pastor, and is doing a stunning job encouraging others who are going through pain.

Look at the process God took her through to prepare her for the job.

I have come to realize that people who go through certain things are able to comfort you easily when they speak with you. Again, God has a way of preparing you for his purpose.

I don't know what your situation is. It might not

be like Ama's. Don't throw in the towel, hold on tight. You will use same to wipe your sweat after celebration.

It is worth noting that "everyone hates suffering, but the fact is pain changes people. It's not meant to make us weak it's to make us stronger. When Christians go through pain in life it helps us to get back on the path of righteousness. We lose all self-reliance and turn to the only one who can help us"(biblereasons.com)

Tim Keller said something profound, "one of the main ways we move from abstract knowledge about God to a personal encounter with him as a living reality is through the furnace of affliction."

Few useful lessons from Ama's story:

- No matter what you are going through, keep trusting God. It doesn't matter what it is. I have personally learnt not to doubt God for anything anymore.

- Do not mess up during the waiting period (be faithful and trust God).The easiest way to delay your waiting period is to walk in sin.

- Fight for what is valuable to you through prayer.

- Stay away from bad company.

- Be careful what advice you take especially when you are in a tough situation.

- Let prayer and your bible be your support system.

I trust that this piece will speak to you and keep you focused and keep you trusting God no matter what your situation is. "For this reason I tell you, whatever you pray and ask for, believe that you have received it, and it will be yours"-Mark 11:24(NET). Art Linkletter serves us well by positing that , "Things turn out best for the people who make the best of the way things work out."

10. House helps

I can write a whole thesis on house helps. Some come to help, others to destroy your beautiful home. Prayer is the only thing that kicks them out.

Some use witchcraft and try causing separation in your lovely homes so that they can be comfortable. Spouses must always be in agreement before helps are brought in, and stay together on issues. This will make their prayer effective. I recently heard of a story of a house help who turned out to be a witch. This came up when their children started having strange dreams, and as a result, the Husband 'fired prayers' one night, and anointed the whole house. He fired prayers directly to the house help's room at midnight, and fasted the following day. After work, he came back home, and while enjoying the company of his wife, the girl rushed in saying she would leave at about 9 pm in the evening. The man 'fired prayers' with his house boy again, and the lady started scratching her whole body as if fire was burning her. She was also gesticulating wildly, as if she was flying. This went on for some time, but she was finally delivered. The following day, she was taken to the station, and off she went.

Can you imagine if someone like this was in your home?

On the other hand, some people have been extremely fortunate to have good house helps. Whatever the case, be on fire!

11. Nagging

Napoleon Hill, in Sixteen Laws of Success, suggests that nagging interferes with chemistry of the mind to such an extent that the individual could lose ambition and gradually sink into oblivion. So please stop nagging if you do, or at best don't start it at all.

12. Selfish spouse

There are instances where both spouses work to earn an income, but one would always like to save his or hers, while the other spouse pays all the bills. In one example that I heard, a wife called her husband in the office through their house help to give her money to buy salt for cooking. The husband pleaded with his wife, through the house help, to buy the salt, and he promised paying when he returned. She agreed. By implication, she had the money but did not want to use it on the family. Why would a spouse not change, if this persists?

13. Art of receiving

There is this story about a man who bought a Vlisco (Holland) cloth to surprise the wife as a Christmas gift. The wife saw the cloth, and said, - "Was this the only color in the shop?

Another incident occurred where a friend went to Woolworth (Ghana) to buy some clothes for the family. She saw a nice pair of jeans, and called the husband to find out what size would suit him. The husband went like "Please send me pictures of the jeans in the shop for me to choose which type I like". What do you think happened to the surprise, and the love with which the woman wanted to shop for the husband?

Couples must learn to appreciate each other, and more importantly, the thought behind the gift. If this art is not learnt, it could breed a lot of problems, and cause spouses to change. Spouses indeed change as indicated earlier, what is important is for each spouse to take feedback, and be willing to improve.

5

REACTIVATNG YOUR MARRIAGE OR MAKING IT WORK

"Always do your best. What you plant now,
you will harvest later"
Og Mandino.

$\mathcal{R}$eflect on your current way of life and its consequences, and ask whether God approves of what you are doing. Ultimately, we are answerable to God as Christians, so we must strive to live per his standards as prescribed in the Bible, tapping into grace.

1. Stop trying to make your marriage work by yourself.

Rely on GOD: through prayer, laboring in the Word, looking out for anointed tapes and books. There is always transference.

2. Confront your issues through communication.

You can pray for 50 million years .If you do not confront your issues, and take responsibility, the issues will never fly away. Find an appropriate place and discuss issues bothering both of you. You might be amazed how easy some of the issues will be resolved. However, both parties must commit to the agreed actions.

3. Speak well - "Death and life is in the

power of the tongue, and those who love it will eat its fruits" Proverbs 18:21. Never think it is not possible to resolve any situation.

Abraham through patience obtained the promise. Whatever you believe will be manifested physically so be careful of what you believe.

Proverbs 14:1

The wisest of women builds her house, but folly with her own hands tears it down.

Proverbs 15:7

The lips of the wise spread knowledge; not so the hearts of fools.

Calm down in an argument, although it is sometimes very difficult and speak well since the bible says it is not what goes in but what comes out that defiles a man.

Caution for men! Dwell with her in an understanding way that your prayers may not be hindered. 1Pet 3:7

1 Peter 3:7

7 Likewise, husbands, live with your wives in an understanding way, showing honor to the woman as the weaker vessel, since they are heirs with you of the grace of life, so that your prayers may not be hindered. (ESV)

Simply put, no matter how your wife is, if you do not treat her well, your prayers will be hindered. I admit this can be tough, especially when you think you are doing your very best. Just strive to do as the holy book says, and God will bless you. If you are able to handle it well, your wife will notice your effort and will do her best to also make changes in herself, to make you happy.

4. Try hard.

As much as practicable, do what makes your spouse happy. Period!

Don't try to always push your spouse to do things your way. If s/he has taken time to discuss an issue with you at least three time, do your best to change.

I know of a situation where a woman will always like to clean her shoes in the car when She and the Husband are going out. The husband hates it because of the dirt that it produces. But she will always repeat it, and when he tries to prompt her to stop, she will explain that there is not much dirt on her shoes. Is this right?

5. The element of surprise.

Surprise your spouse with gifts. A gift makes room for men……. Become positively unpredictable, but spouses must learn the art of receiving to encourage their spouses to do more.

6. Take a trip together

A trip together spices up your relationship in a remarkable way. The trip must not necessarily be abroad. It could be a locally planned get away with the whole family or your spouse alone. Some people even take advantage of funerals to do this.

It changes everything – communication, love

making etc. The bonding is simply worth the trip. A trip together fires up exciting elements in the relationship in a unique way.

7. Give quality hugs

Give quality hugs because it is a form of physical intimacy. Touch gives positive vibes in a relationship.

A good hug is an emotional thing. It indicates familiarity, love, affection, friendship etc. According to Wikipedia, it demonstrates affection and emotional warmth, sometimes arising from joy or happiness.

8.   Hold each other very tight when you are   sleeping / making love: this bonds you   together

9.   Make LOVE, and in the process kiss and touch everywhere. This soften hearts. Love making is a spiritual thing. When it is well done, it bonds the couple in a unique way and also generates an inexplicable excitement.

Most women think it is only women who like to be kissed everywhere. What is good for the goose is good for the gander. Let your man also know you care

10. Know the strengths and weaknesses of your partners, and try to accept them with a very big heart.

11. Seek a role model.
A role model should be someone you look up to or are accountable to. This has been of tremendous help to me. Kindly let me use this opportunity to thank Dr. and Mrs. Agyapong for helping us grow in marriage.

12. Don't compare your spouse with a friend.
One of the things that can degenerate a relationship quickly is comparison. Enjoy what you have and stay focused. Most people do not give the full details of what pertains in their relationship. They only tell you the nice things.

Stay glued to your spouse and grow what you

have and try to limit what you say about your relationship to others.

13. Try giving each other the benefit of the doubt. Assume the best for each other.
The Key is expecting good outcomes from each other. It is important not to assume after an argument with your spouse that your marriage is doomed. Conflicts are good in any healthy relationship. It all depends on how they are handled. *"Conflict is therapeutic"* Robert Greene.

14. Celebrate small positive changes in your relationship.
 It reinforces learning, and encourages repetition or improvement.

15. Let go of your ex if it makes your spouse uncomfortable.
It is important to leave nothing to feed his/her fears, especially if   your spouse struggles with jealously.

16. One of the quickest ways to reactivate your marriage or make it work is to find out who speaks into the life of your spouse?

Some people are simply negative influences. All they do is to compound the issues you have by speaking about negative things and as per the law of attraction, which says "Like attracts like".

This philosophy is used to sum up the idea that by focusing on positive or negative thoughts, a person brings positive or negative experiences into their life. Wikipedia

If you want to experience a positive relationship, only say/focus on positive things about your relationship / spouse.

6

BLIND SPOT

"spirituality is the root of all profiting".

Bishop David Oyedepo

Whereas so many people are getting divorced, others are living in pain and pretending all is well.

A brother shared a phenomenal story with me about his marriage. He said every time he wanted to make love with his wife, it always ended up in confusion or from one argument to another (I like this; I like it this way...) until each of them got frustrated. He resorted to dealing with it through prayer. This led him to see someone standing behind one of the curtains in their bedroom, in a dream. He picked up an item, and struck the person behind the curtain very hard. The person fell, and changed into a snake that was badly hurt. The snake split into two from the waist level down. The top half, i.e. from head to waist started to run for its life. When the man woke up, he prayed about the dream, and in a trance he saw that the snake was struggling to run away. He dealt with it through prayer (Holy Ghost Fire!) until the snake died. A few days later, they made love, and he satisfied her like never before.

The thing I want to share with you, in addition to all that I have shared so far, is that, this gentleman for instance might have assumed that all he was going through was physical, but it was more spiritual than he could ever imagine. He kept doing his part, but it was still tough.

"Your spiritual battles are the root cause of all your problems. There is no one who is not fighting a spiritual battle." -Bishop Oyedepo.

We inherit curses and blessings through covenants that we know nothing about. Our ability therefore to claim the covenants or break the curses will determine how far we go in life.

Some people claim that if you are in Christ you are a new creation. But I tell you, people with even higher anointing are praying, but still working hard at their marriages. You need both.

Let me support my assertion above with a few scriptures below. I have underlined where I want to place emphasis.

Gen 6:18

18 But I will establish my covenant with you, and you shall come into the ark, you, your <u>sons</u>, your <u>wife</u>, and your <u>sons' wives</u> with you.(ESV)

Gen 13:14-15

14 The Lord said to Abram, after Lot had separated from him, "Lift up your eyes and look from the place where you are, northward and southward and eastward and westward,

15 for all the land that you see I will give to you and to <u>your offspring forever.</u>(ESV)

Ezk 24:21

21 'Say to the house of Israel, Thus says the Lord God: Behold, I will profane my sanctuar y, the pride of your power, the delight of your eyes, and the yearning of your soul, and <u>your sons</u> and <u>your daughters</u> whom you left behind shall fall by the *sword.(ESV)*

Dan 6:24

24 And the king commanded, and those men who had maliciously accused Daniel were brought and cast into the den of lions—they, <u>their children,</u> and <u>their wives.</u> And before they reached the bottom of the den, the lions over powered them and broke all their bones in pieces.(ESV)

This is a true indication of how our spouses, children/offspring, and even son's wives inherit blessings or curses. So beware! Mind you, you need to do your bit with your prayers and giving. None should stand alone.

On this note, I declare that, whatever wants to challenge your future or present marriage situation/relationship shall be cut off from today, in the name of Jesus!

7

FINAL THOUGHTS

"The young man knows the rules, but the old man knows the exceptions".

Jurist Oliver Wendell Holmes

$\mathcal{I}$ personally believe there are stages in marriage. When the stages are understood, and what to expect at each stage is known, it makes the marriage smoother. Seek to know and understand these stages.

However, the true foundation of a lasting relationship is the grace of God. That is the one and only differentiator. It is also very important to make right choices from the onset. Look at where you are going, and look for a spouse who matches where you are going.

Nobody is perfect. Spouses should therefore strive to get better through personal development. It is said that growth is not automatic but intentional: **read** books on marriage, **feed** on the Bible, **pray**, **reflect**, **listen** to tapes, **attend** seminars, **get** role models or counselors who can speak into your lives, **visit** YouTube. These are simple keys that will help you develop. If you do not invest in yourself, do not expect to get a return on your marriage -period!

Marriage is indeed an important aspect of our personal development which most people neglect. Consequently, most people have made mistakes that could have been avoided, and they continue to make mistakes and keep learning on the job. Someone said something that struck me. He said, "Practice does not make perfect." It is practice with appropriate feedback that makes perfect. Don't be one of those who end up miserable and lonely, hurting and denying their children in the process, by not developing this area of your life.

" *Imagine life as a game in which you are juggling some five balls in the air. You name them - Work, Family, Health, Friends and Spirit, and you're keeping all of these in the air.*

You will soon understand that work is a rubber ball. If you drop it, it will bounce back. But the other four balls

Family, Health, Friends and Spirit - are made of glass. If you drop one of these, they will be irrevocably scuffed, marked, nicked, damaged or even shattered. They will never be the same. You must understand that and strive for it.

Work efficiently during office hours and leave on time. Give the required time to your family, friends and have proper rest. Value has a value only if its value is valued."

Bryan Dyson - Former CEO of Coca Cola.

A good marriage is a legacy that we leave for our children, to see, and to follow. Can your children and those around you, truly look at you and model their marriage according to yours? This is a goal anyone who wants to leave a legacy worth living should strive for. It is tough but with God all things are possible.

Stay Super Blessed!

About The Author

Deladem Komla Loglo is a Banker, Personal Development Consultant. He is the Founder of Yang Steps Consulting. He holds a Bsc. in Development Planning from KNUST and MBA in Marketing from UCC.

He started his career with Unilever, moved on to Barclays and occupied several roles within a span of five years six months: Sales Manager, Senior Sales Manager, Head of Bancassurance, Premier Relationship Manager. He also managed three of the Largest Branches in Barclays Ghana i.e. High Street, Circle and Osu Branches. He is currently a Territorial Unit Head @ SG Ghana Limited leading seven key Branches of the Bank.

Deladem has a solid record for accomplishing both corporate and personal goals. With his multi-disciplinary background and training, he is well grounded in sales, entrepreneurship, and leadership and excels in roles that require people management. He has clearly demonstrated the ability to head multiple large units, and as such, he developed a lot of people during his career. He is always seeking an opportunity to learn and add value to himself and the people he leads.

Deladem believes his purpose in life is to impact and become a blessing to anybody who comes into his life. Therefore, he is passionate about sharing practical insights with others, so that they may live balanced lives.

Deladem is married to an incredible wife, Aseye and blessed with three adorable children

Connect with the author

https://www.facebook.com/deladem.loglo

https://www.instagram.com/delademloglo

Origin Of Name

Yin and Yang are two complementary principles of Chinese philosophy:

Yin is negative, dark, and feminine. Yang is positive, bright, and masculine. their interaction is thought to maintain the harmony of the universe and to influence everything within it.

Yang steps consulting was derived by twisting young to yang. we believe that though yin and yang are complementary, yang alone will stand in the name of Jesus and by the power of the holy ghost.

Who We Are

A global personal development consultancy with a single purpose: to share practical insights with individuals to unleash their potential to live balanced lives.

What We Do

- Personal Development Consultants
- Event organizers
- Corporate Trainers
- Production and Distribution of Educational Material

Mission

To help people believe their destiny is in their own hands

Biblical Foundation

"Now lift up your eyes and look from the place where you are, northward and southward and eastward and westward; 15 for all the land which you see, I will give it to you and to your descendants forever".

Genesis 13:14 -15

Target Group:

Students, Professionals and Entrepreneurs.

Segment	Target Group	Positioning
Students	Senior High up to National Service	Yang Students Series
Professionals	Young Professionals in the Corporate world who aspire to quickly accelerate to the top in their careers, or people with aspirations of becoming entrepreneurs	Yang Executive Series
Entrepreneurs	People who have started their own businesses who require help to transform their businesses I individuals who have a business idea and want to see it made manifest.	Yang Entrepreneurs Series

Core Values

a. Passion

b. Continuous learning

c. Excellence

d. Integrity

Differentiation

• Practical insights and Biblical foundation

Contact Us

P.O Box AT 1508, Achimota - Market, Accra

Talk to us on: **(+233) 20 2019599, (+233) 24 4209871**

Facebook:

www.facebook.com/yangstepscons ulting

Email:

yangstepsconsulting@gmail.com

Website:

www.yangstepsconsulting.com

NOTE...

<u>NOTE</u>...

www.ingramcontent.com/pod-product-compliance
Lightning Source LLC
Chambersburg PA
CBHW060446160726
47992CB00003B/1101